1

Forests covered a lot of Australia.

3

Possums lived in the forest.
Possums were food for the First
People.

5

Possum fur was very warm. The fur was made into coats.

7

Some forests were rainforests.
Other forests were very dry.

9

The First People lived in the forests. The trees were used for making many things.

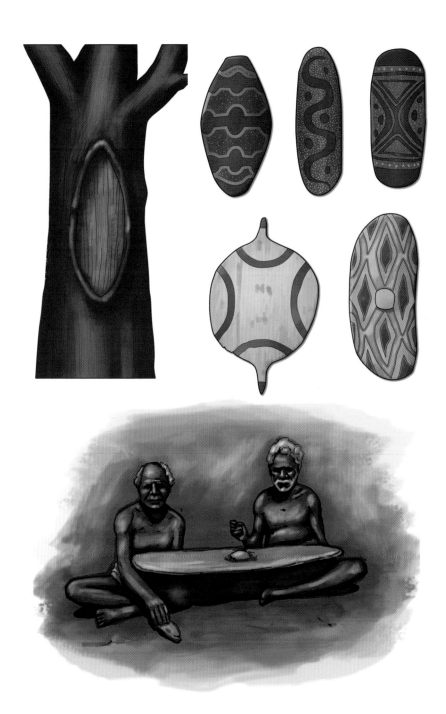

The First People would follow tracks through the forest.

13

The forests grew around many lakes.

15

There were forests on the coast.
These forests are called
mangroves.

17

Fish need forests for fresh water.
Fish can live in mangroves.

19

Forests had many trees which had fruit and seeds.

21

The forests had many birds.
This is a kookaburra.

23

Word bank

forests

Australia

possum

coats

rainforests

mangroves

things

tracks

grew

around

lakes

coast

water

kookaburra